SCHIRMER'S LIBRARY
OF MUSICAL CLASSICS

Vol. 2022

MAURICE RAVEL

Selected Short Masterpieces

including *Le Tombeau de Couperin and Valses Nobles et Sentimentales*

For Piano

ISBN 978-0-7935-6290-9

G. SCHIRMER, Inc.

DISTRIBUTED BY

HAL•LEONARD®
CORPORATION
7777 W. BLUEMOUND RD. P.O. BOX 13819 MILWAUKEE, WI 53213

CONTENTS

ANTIQUE MINUET

Maurice Ravel

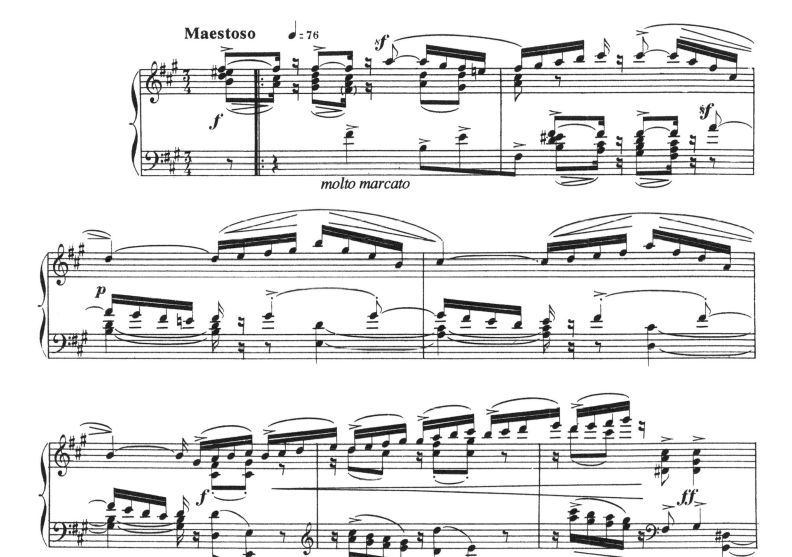

Una corda

mf

sf

(Tre corde)

pp

U.C.

mf

sf

(T.C.)

mp

mf

L.H.   R.H.

f

p   L.H.

ff

sf   sf

4

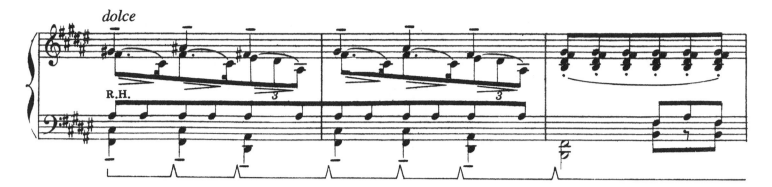

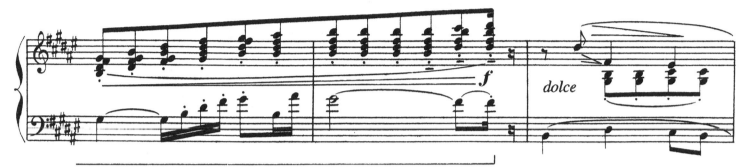

Pocchissimo più lento

Rallentando

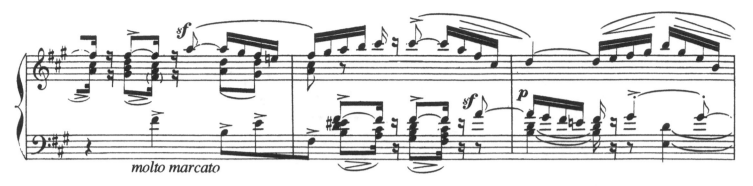

molto marcato

molto deciso

pp

Una corda

(T.C.)

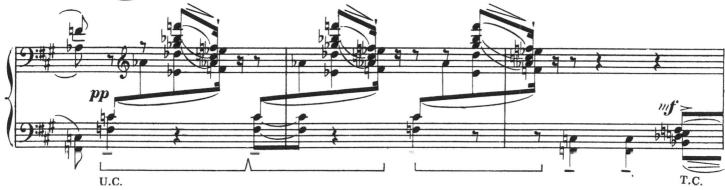

PAVANE
in memory of an Infanta

Maurice Ravel

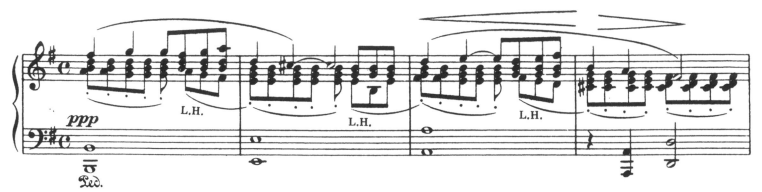

poco più lento

A tempo

Rall. *rapide* **A tempo**

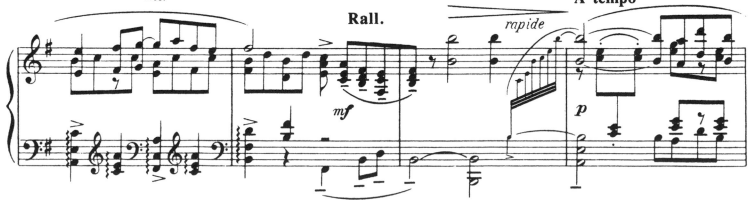

poco ritenuto **Largo**

subito

in fuori la melodia

MINUET
on the name of Haydn

Maurice Ravel

Tempo di Minuetto

VALSES NOBLES ET SENTIMENTALES

*"...the ever-renewed delight
of a useless pastime."*

(Henri de Regnier)

Maurice Ravel

I

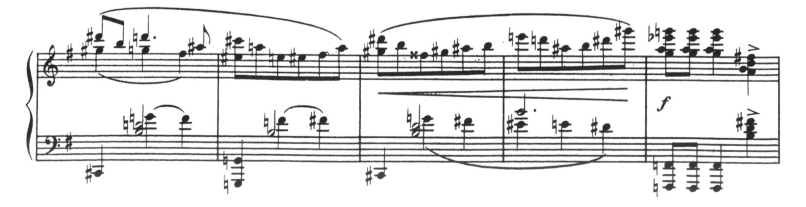

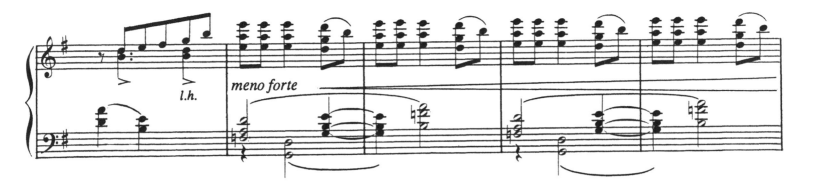

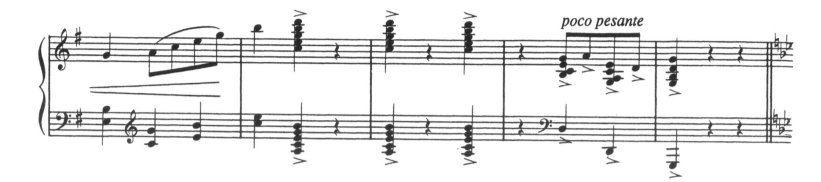

II

Lento assai—with intense expression ♩ = 104

in relief

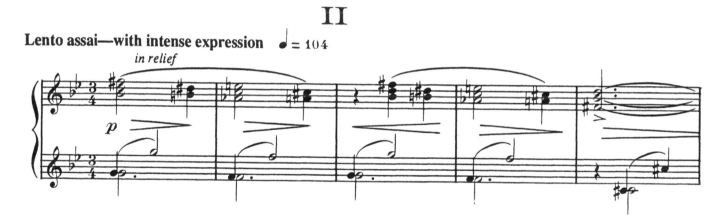

Rit.   **a Tempo**
dolce ed espressivo

A tempo (poco piu lento e rubato)

espressivo

A tempo primo

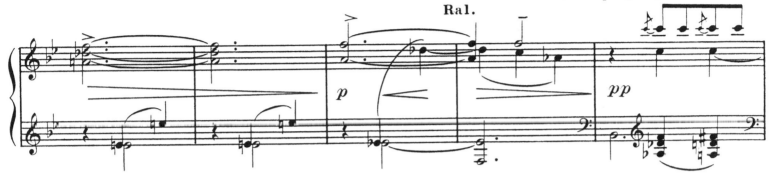

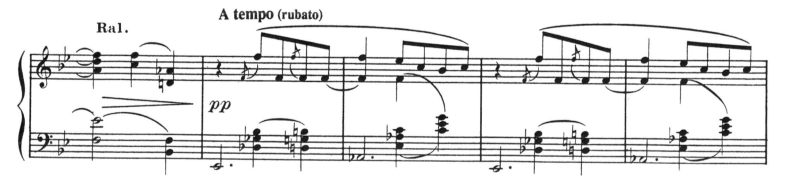

III

Moderato

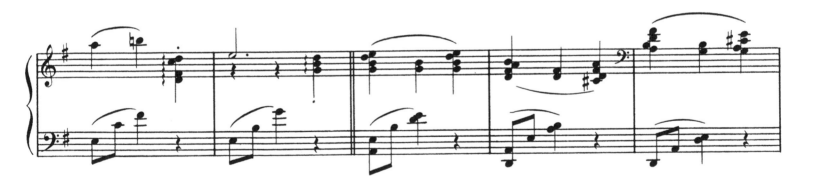

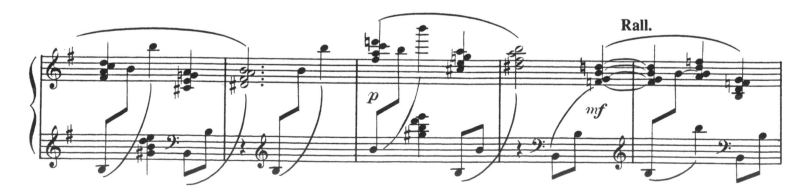

A tempo

molto espressivo   **Rallentando**

A tempo

pp   *sostenuto*

Ritenuto

IV

Animato assai ♩. = 80

Pocchissimo rall. **A tempo**

slightly in relief

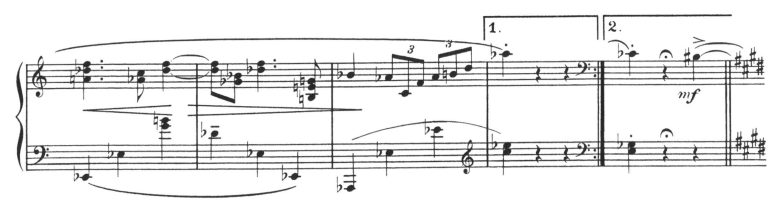

V

Quasi lento—intimate in feeling $\quad \bullet = 96$

top line strongly in relief

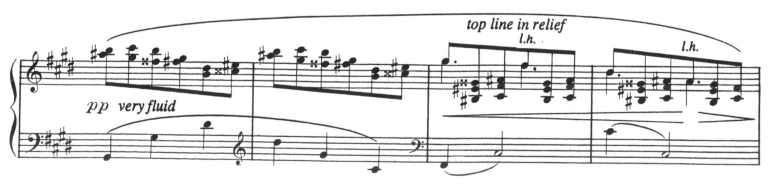

VI

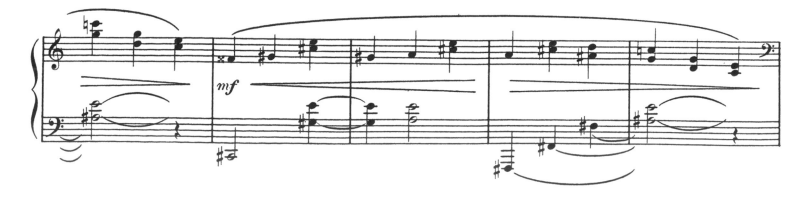

Rallentando

A tempo

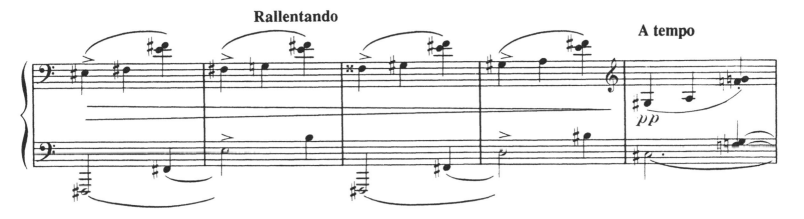

Pocchissimo rall. **A tempo**

very soft and somewhat languishing

VII

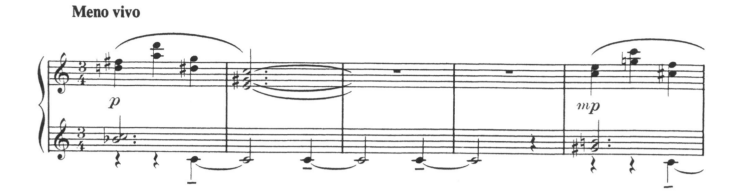

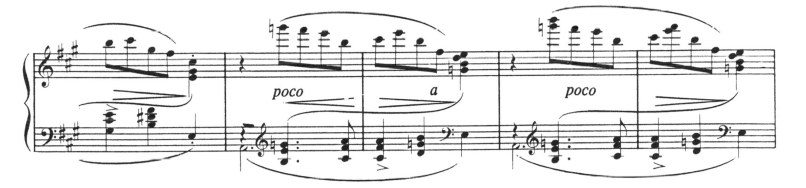

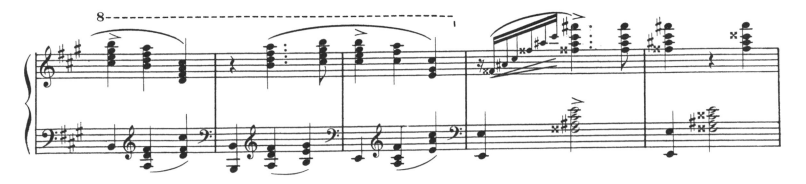

Poco ritenuto   **A tempo**

Poco più animato

dolcissimo, top line in relief

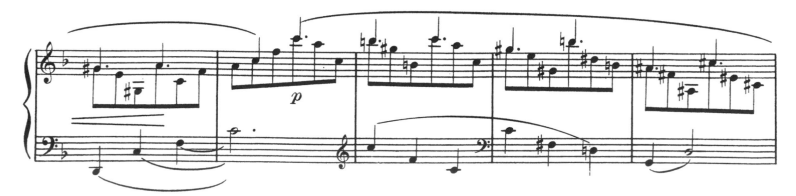

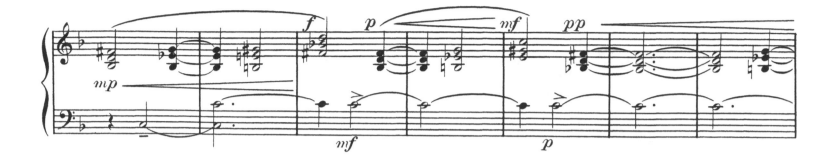

Tempo primo

espressivo

slightly in relief

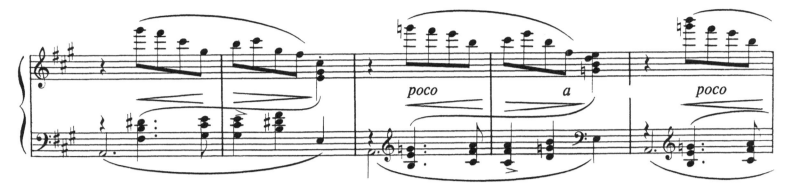

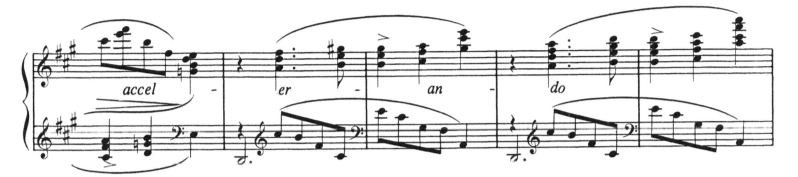

Poco ritenuto   A tempo

VIII

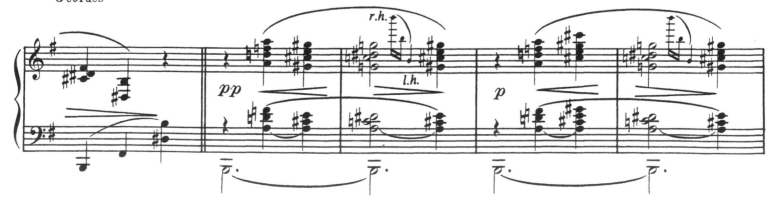

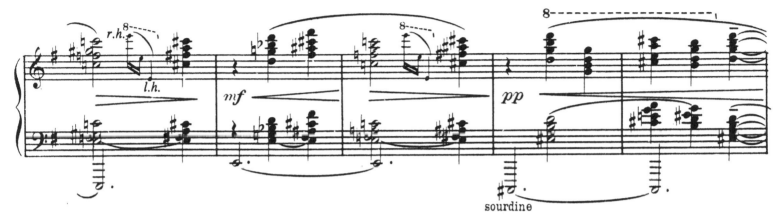

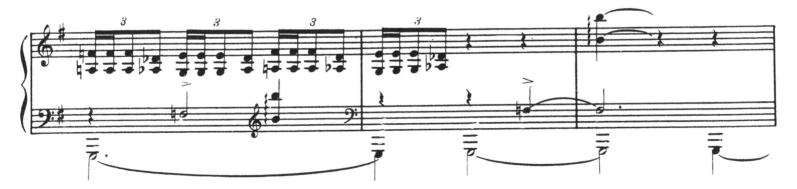

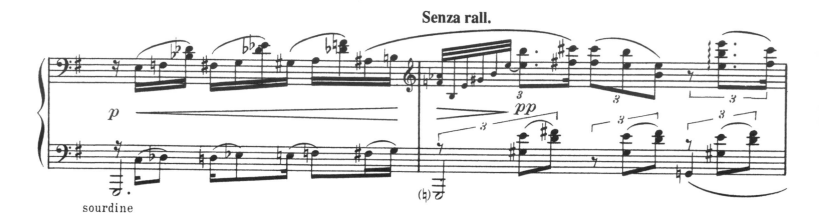

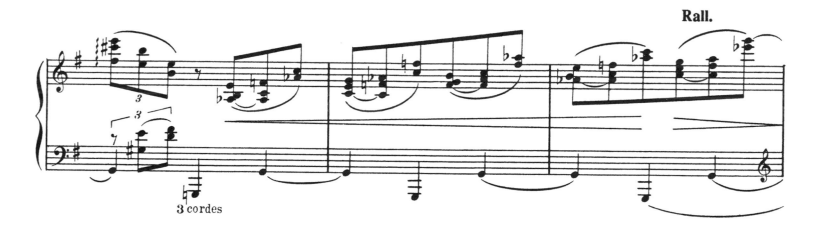

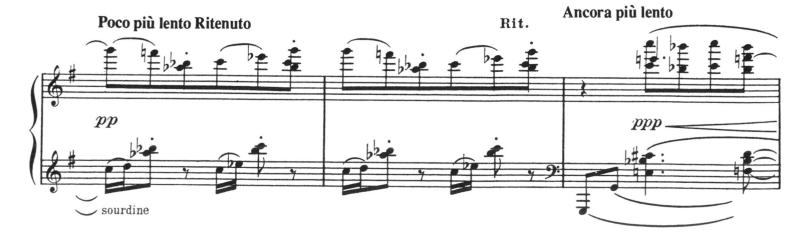

PRELUDE

Maurice Ravel

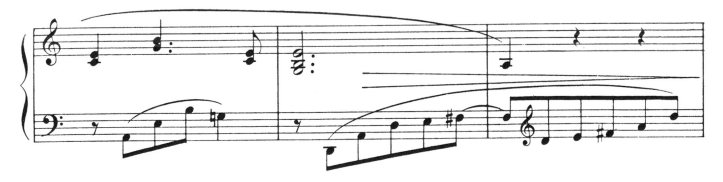

Ritenuto   **A tempo**

Ritenuto

Molto lento

IN THE STYLE OF ...

Borodin

Valse

Maurice Ravel

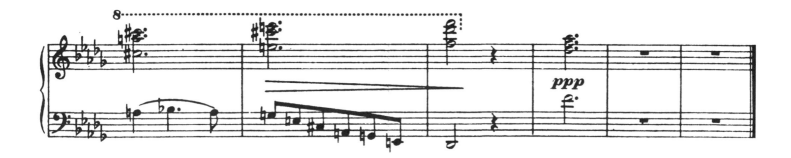

Emmanuel Chabrier

Paraphrase on an air by Gounod (Faust Act. II)

MAURICE RAVEL

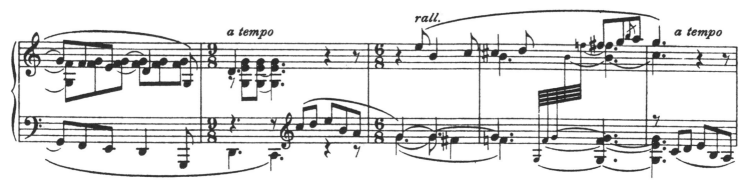

to the memory of Lieutenant Jacques Charlot

LE TOMBEAU DE COUPERIN

I. Prelude

Maurice Ravel

*The grace notes are to be struck on the beat.

49

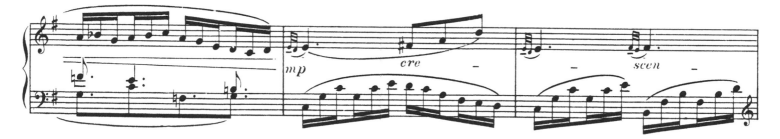

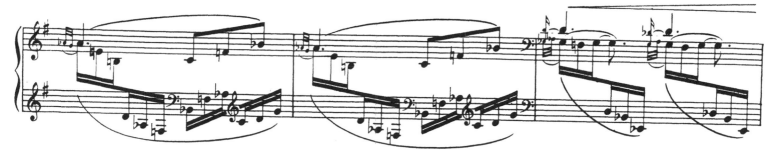

to the memory of Second Lieutenant Jean Cruppi

II. Fugue

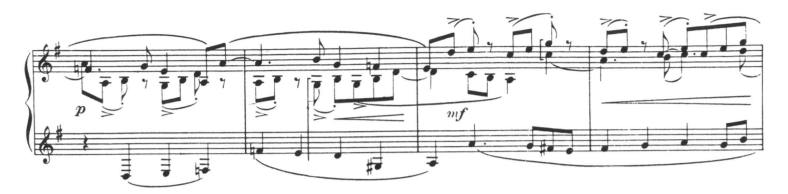

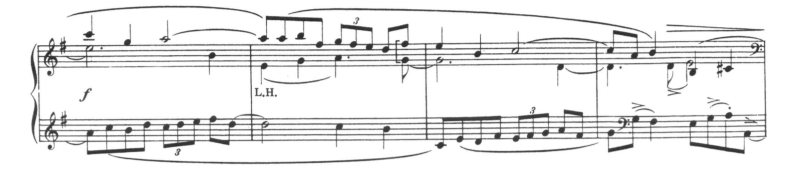

to the memory of Lieutenant Gabriel Deluc

III. Forlane

*The grace notes are to be struck on the beat.

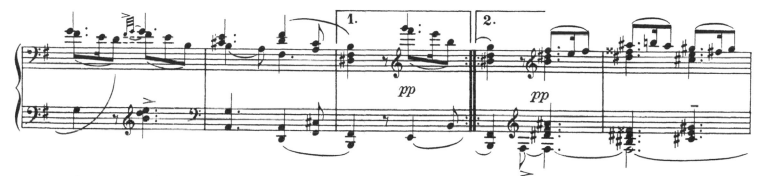

Senza rallentare

to the memory of Pierre and Pascal Gaudin

IV. Rigaudon

*The grace notes are to be struck on the beat.

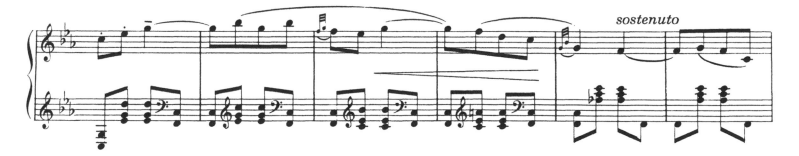

Una corda

Tre corde

U.c.

Tempo I

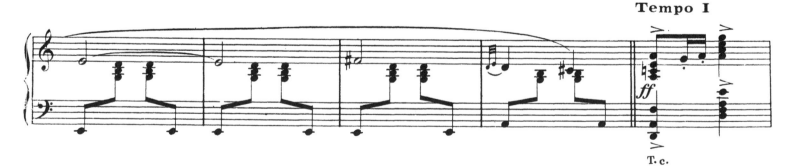

T.c.

to the memory of Jean Dreyfus

V. Menuet

*The grace notes are to be struck on the beat.

Una corda

Musette

pp

Una corda

Tre corde

p

mf

ff

poco dim.

f

mf sostenuto

pp

Una corda

to the memory of Captain Joseph de Marliave

VI. Toccata

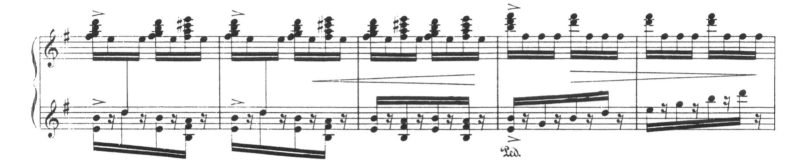

72

Poco meno vivo

sostenuto

Tornare al...   Tempo I

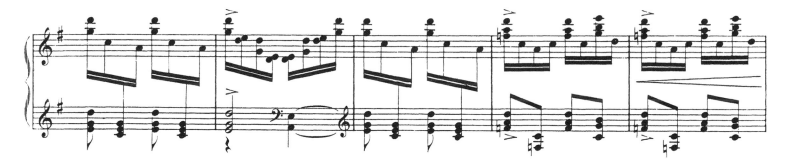

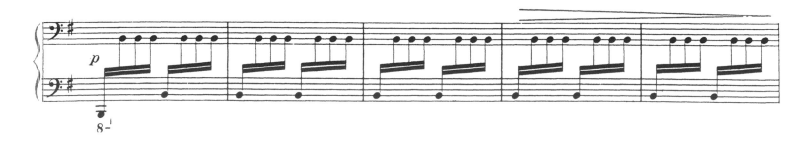

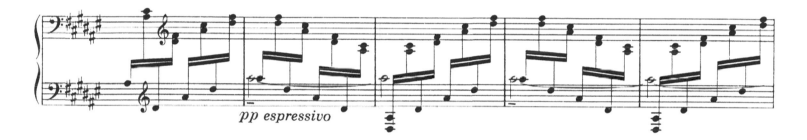

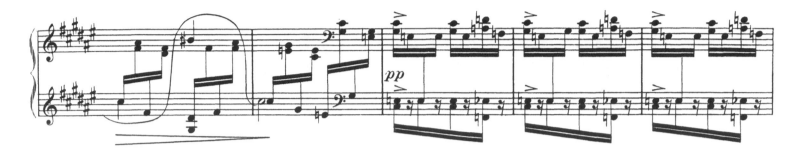

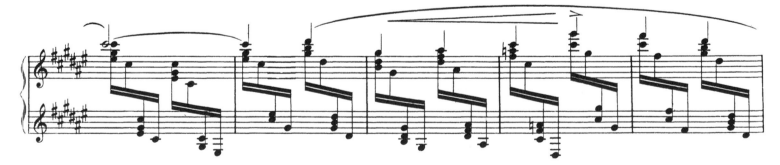

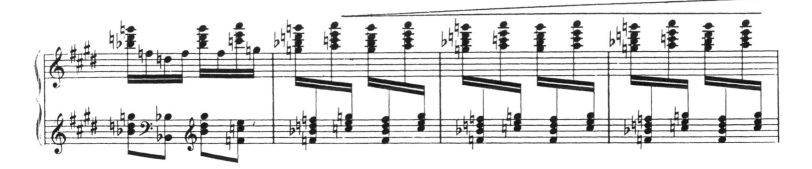

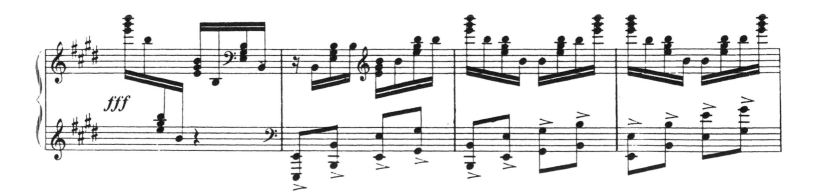

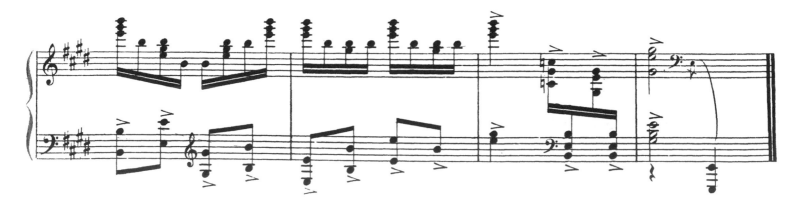